At Inspirio we love to hear from you—your stories, your
feedback, and your product ideas. Please send your comments
to us by way of e-mail at icares@zondervan.com

Requests for information should be addressed to:
Inspirio, The gift group of Zondervan
Grand Rapids, Michigan 49530
http://www.inspiriogifts.com

Compiler: Julie Sutton
Editor: Janice Jacobson
Project Manager: Patti Matthews
Design: Mark Veldheer
Photography: Synergy Photographic
Photo stylist: Jan Bridgeman

Printed in China
03 04 05/HK/ 4 3 2 1

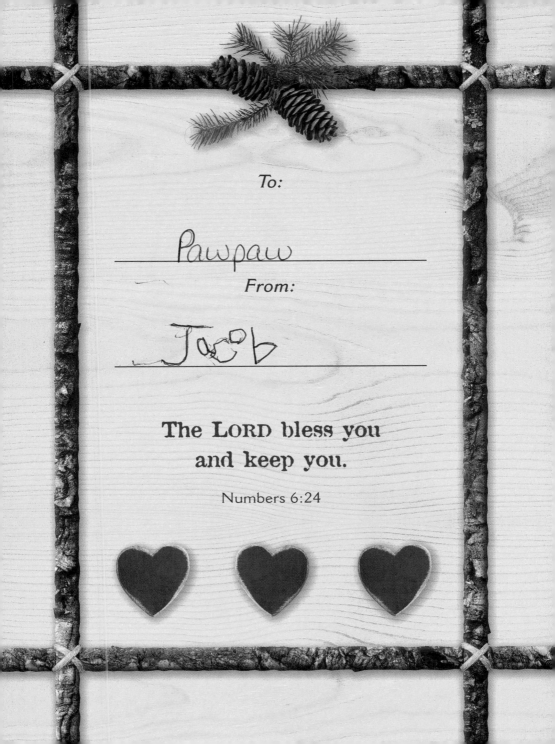

To:

Pawpaw

From:

Jacob

The LORD bless you and keep you.

Numbers 6:24

**May the LORD give you the
desire of your heart and
make all your plans succeed.**

Psalm 20:4

*You will go out in joy
and be led forth in peace;
the mountains and hills
will burst into song before you,
and all the trees of the field
will clap their hands.*

Isaiah 55:12

May the LORD grant all your requests.

Psalm 20:5

You, O LORD, keep my lamp burning;
my God turns my darkness into light.

Psalm 18:28

Many, O LORD my God,
are the wonders you have done.
The things you planned for us
no one can recount to you;
were I to speak and tell of them,
they would be too many to declare.

Psalm 40:5

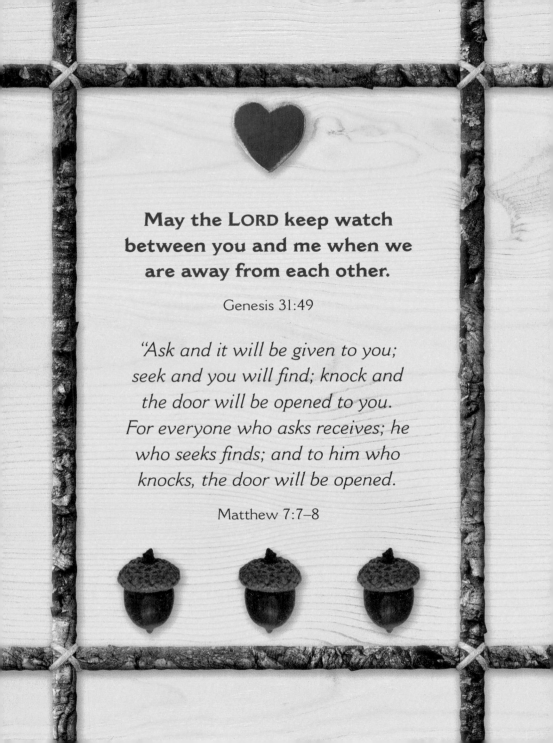

May the LORD keep watch between you and me when we are away from each other.

Genesis 31:49

"Ask and it will be given to you; seek and you will find; knock and the door will be opened to you. For everyone who asks receives; he who seeks finds; and to him who knocks, the door will be opened.

Matthew 7:7–8

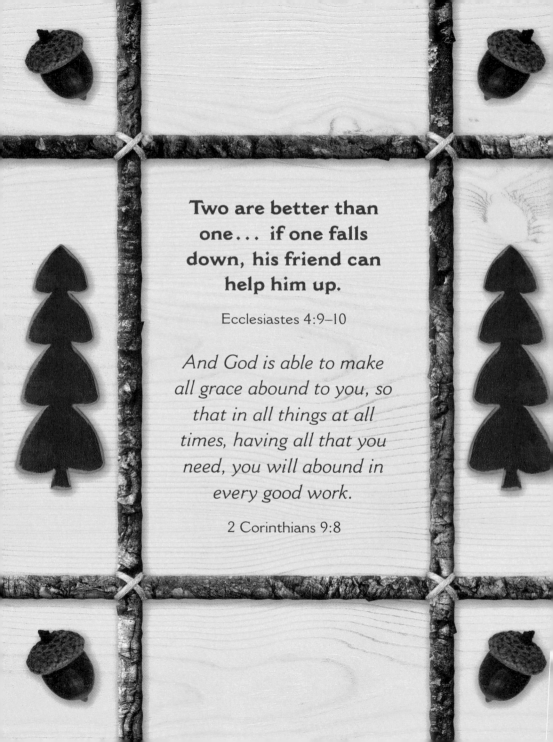

Two are better than one... if one falls down, his friend can help him up.

Ecclesiastes 4:9–10

And God is able to make all grace abound to you, so that in all things at all times, having all that you need, you will abound in every good work.

2 Corinthians 9:8

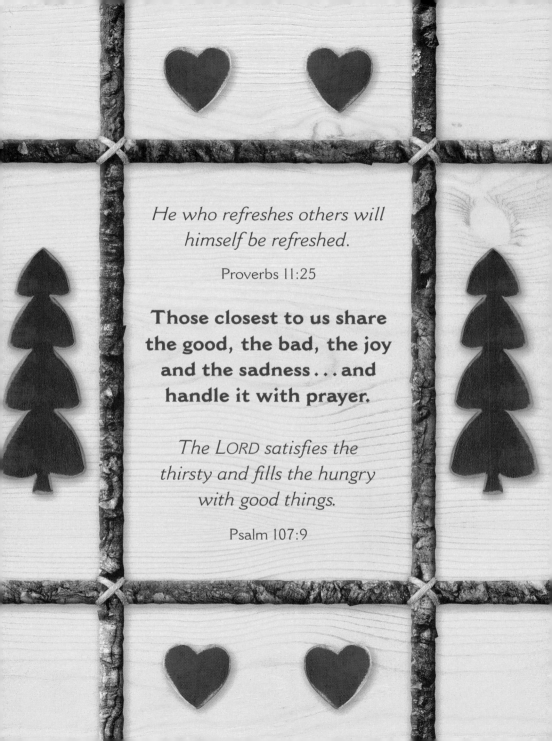

He who refreshes others will
himself be refreshed.

Proverbs 11:25

**Those closest to us share
the good, the bad, the joy
and the sadness . . . and
handle it with prayer.**

*The LORD satisfies the
thirsty and fills the hungry
with good things.*

Psalm 107:9

Be still and know that I am God.

Psalm 46:10

Away from the cares of everyday life, we find a place to be more truly who we are, and who we were truly meant to be.

Now may the Lord of peace himself give you peace at all times and in every way.

2 Thessalonians 3:16

God's love is everywhere, but shines especially bright in the eyes of those close to our hearts.

Your love, O LORD, reaches the heavens, your faithfulness to the skies.

Psalm 36:5

Hearts are truly joined when Jesus lives inside them.

Delight yourself in the LORD and he will give you the desires or your heart.

Psalm 37:4

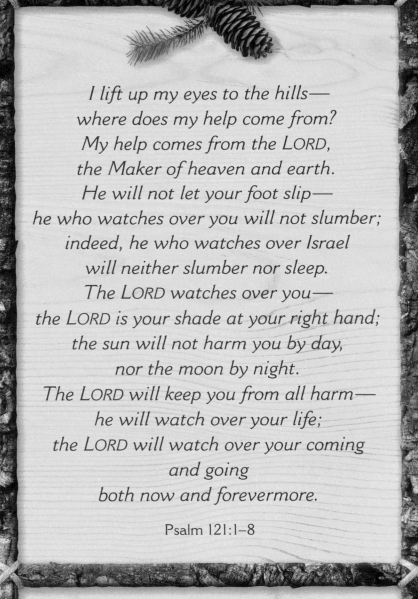

I lift up my eyes to the hills—
where does my help come from?
My help comes from the LORD,
the Maker of heaven and earth.
He will not let your foot slip—
he who watches over you will not slumber;
indeed, he who watches over Israel
will neither slumber nor sleep.
The LORD watches over you—
the LORD is your shade at your right hand;
the sun will not harm you by day,
nor the moon by night.
The LORD will keep you from all harm—
he will watch over your life;
the LORD will watch over your coming
and going
both now and forevermore.

Psalm 121:1–8

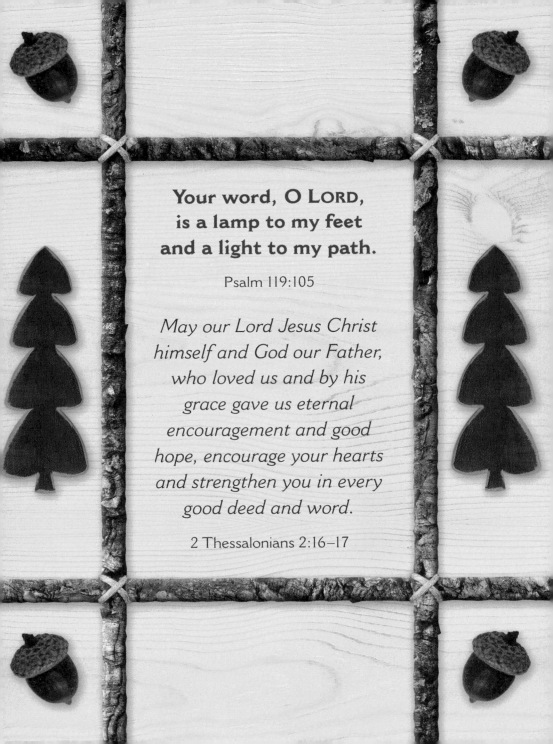

**Your word, O LORD,
is a lamp to my feet
and a light to my path.**

Psalm 119:105

*May our Lord Jesus Christ
himself and God our Father,
who loved us and by his
grace gave us eternal
encouragement and good
hope, encourage your hearts
and strengthen you in every
good deed and word.*

2 Thessalonians 2:16–17

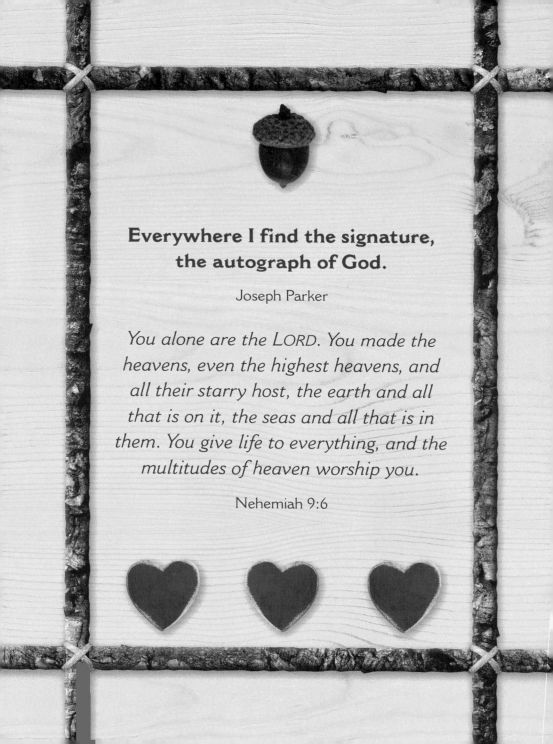

**Everywhere I find the signature,
the autograph of God.**

Joseph Parker

*You alone are the LORD. You made the
heavens, even the highest heavens, and
all their starry host, the earth and all
that is on it, the seas and all that is in
them. You give life to everything, and the
multitudes of heaven worship you.*

Nehemiah 9:6

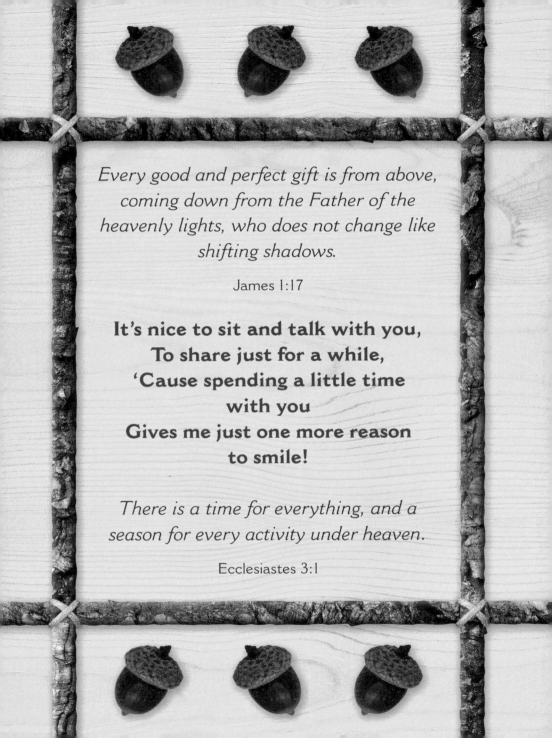

Every good and perfect gift is from above, coming down from the Father of the heavenly lights, who does not change like shifting shadows.

James 1:17

**It's nice to sit and talk with you,
To share just for a while,
'Cause spending a little time
with you
Gives me just one more reason
to smile!**

There is a time for everything, and a season for every activity under heaven.

Ecclesiastes 3:1

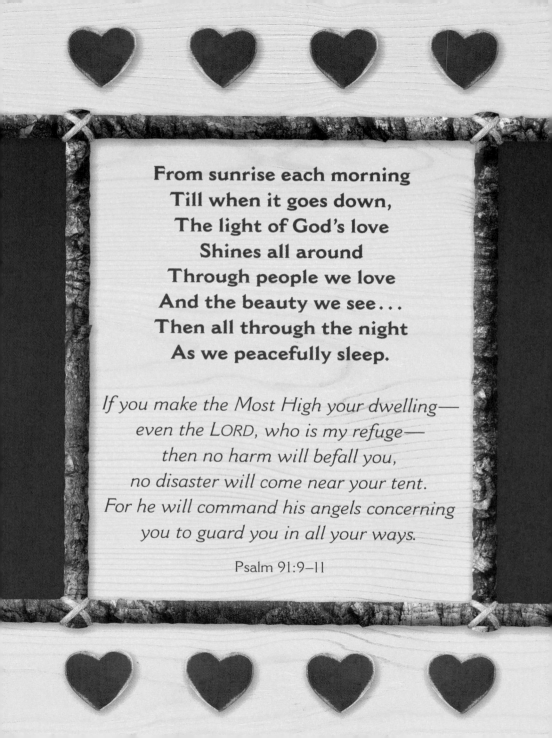

From sunrise each morning
Till when it goes down,
The light of God's love
Shines all around
Through people we love
And the beauty we see...
Then all through the night
As we peacefully sleep.

If you make the Most High your dwelling—
even the LORD, who is my refuge—
then no harm will befall you,
no disaster will come near your tent.
For he will command his angels concerning
you to guard you in all your ways.

Psalm 91:9–11

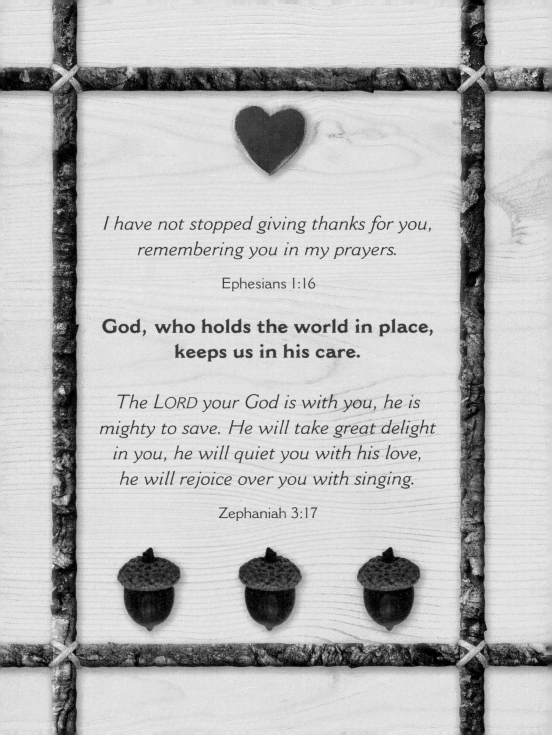

I have not stopped giving thanks for you, remembering you in my prayers.

Ephesians 1:16

God, who holds the world in place, keeps us in his care.

The LORD your God is with you, he is mighty to save. He will take great delight in you, he will quiet you with his love, he will rejoice over you with singing.

Zephaniah 3:17

God will meet all your needs
according to his glorious
riches in Christ Jesus.

Philippians 4:19

**All beauty is a reflection
of the Creator, and all
love springs from his
own endless supply.**

Your Father knows what you
need before you ask him.

Matthew 6:8

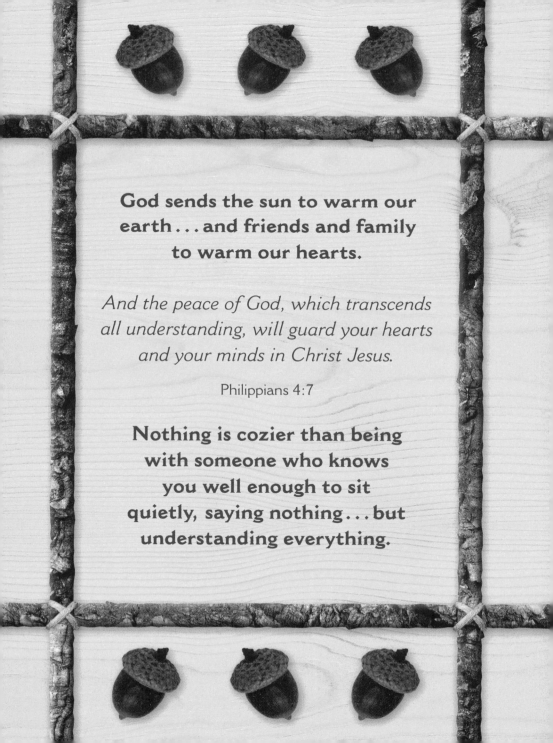

God sends the sun to warm our
earth . . . and friends and family
to warm our hearts.

*And the peace of God, which transcends
all understanding, will guard your hearts
and your minds in Christ Jesus.*

Philippians 4:7

Nothing is cozier than being
with someone who knows
you well enough to sit
quietly, saying nothing . . . but
understanding everything.

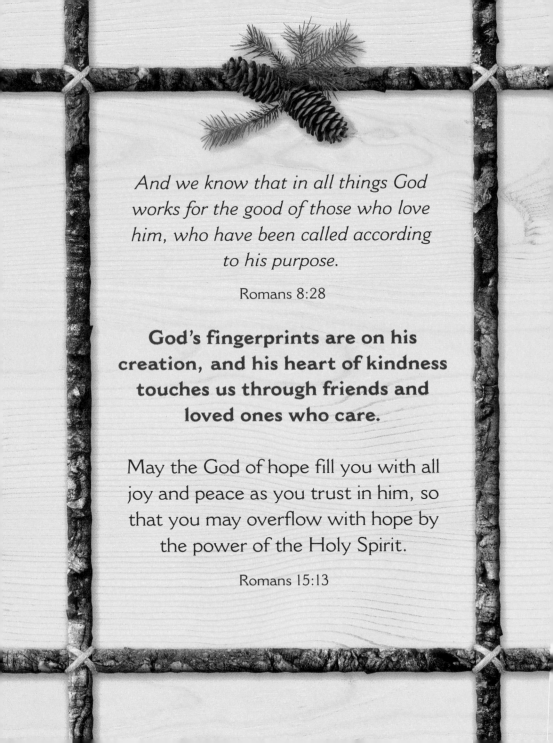

And we know that in all things God works for the good of those who love him, who have been called according to his purpose.

Romans 8:28

God's fingerprints are on his creation, and his heart of kindness touches us through friends and loved ones who care.

May the God of hope fill you with all joy and peace as you trust in him, so that you may overflow with hope by the power of the Holy Spirit.

Romans 15:13

The spacious firmament on high,
With all the blue ethereal sky,
And spangled heavens,
A shining frame.
Their great Original proclaim.
Forever singing, as they shine,
The hand that made us is divine.

Joseph Addison

Lift your eyes and look to the heavens:
Who created all these?
He who brings out the starry host one by
one, and calls them each by name.
Because of his great power and mighty
strength, not one of them is missing.

Isaiah 40:26

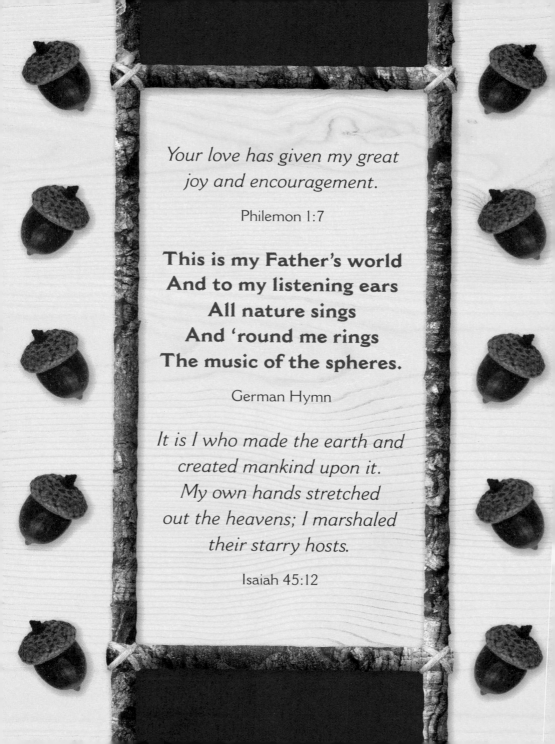

Your love has given my great joy and encouragement.

Philemon 1:7

**This is my Father's world
And to my listening ears
All nature sings
And 'round me rings
The music of the spheres.**

German Hymn

It is I who made the earth and created mankind upon it. My own hands stretched out the heavens; I marshaled their starry hosts.

Isaiah 45:12

May you be blessed by the LORD, the Maker of heaven and earth.

Psalm 115:15

The LORD will endure as long as the sun, as long as the moon, through all generations. He will be like rain falling on a mown field, like showers watering the earth.

Psalm 72:5–6

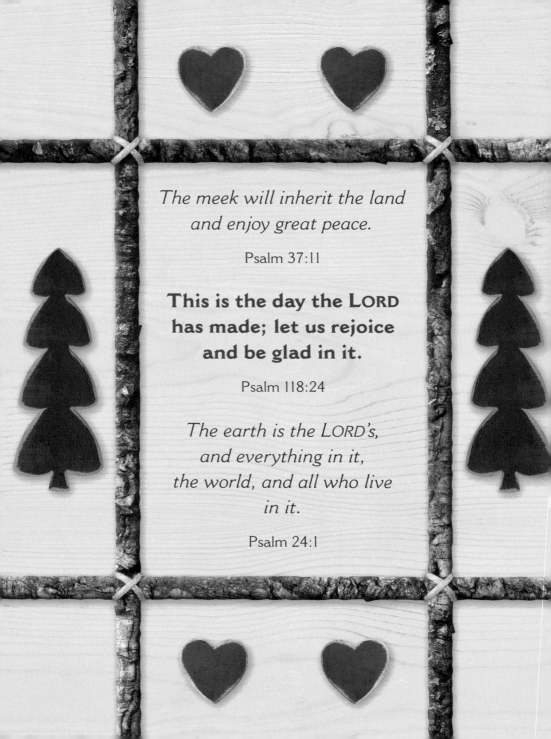

*The meek will inherit the land
and enjoy great peace.*

Psalm 37:11

**This is the day the LORD
has made; let us rejoice
and be glad in it.**

Psalm 118:24

*The earth is the LORD's,
and everything in it,
the world, and all who live
in it.*

Psalm 24:1